Turtles

by Grace Hansen

ABDO
REPTILES
Kids

www.abdopublishing.com

Published by Abdo Kids, a division of ABDO, P.O. Box 398166, Minneapolis, Minnesota 55439.

Copyright © 2015 by Abdo Consulting Group, Inc. International copyrights reserved in all countries. No part of this book may be reproduced in any form without written permission from the publisher.

Printed in the United States of America, North Mankato, Minnesota.

052014

092014

 THIS BOOK CONTAINS RECYCLED MATERIALS

Photo Credits: Glow Images, Shutterstock, Thinkstock

Production Contributors: Teddy Borth, Jennie Forsberg, Grace Hansen

Design Contributors: Candice Keimig, Laura Rask, Dorothy Toth

Library of Congress Control Number: 2013952083

Cataloging-in-Publication Data

Hansen, Grace.

  Turtles / Grace Hansen.

    p. cm. -- (Reptiles)

ISBN 978-1-62970-062-5 (lib. bdg.)

Includes bibliographical references and index.

1. Turtles--Juvenile literature.   I. Title.

597.9--dc23

                    2013952083

Table of Contents

Turtles 4

Turtle Shells 14

Baby Turtles 18

More Facts 22

Glossary 23

Index 24

Abdo Kids Code. 24

Turtles

Turtles are reptiles.

All reptiles have **scales**

and are **cold-blooded**.

5

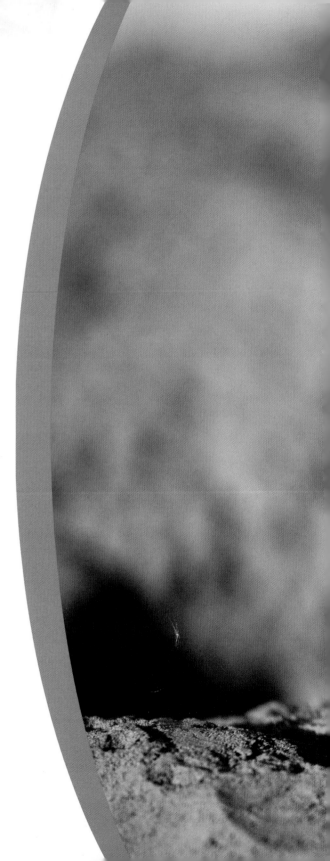

Turtles live in many different **habitats**. Some live in deserts. Others live in forests or mountains.

6

Turtles come in many sizes. Some can weigh as little as 1 pound (0.5 kg).

Some turtles can be very big. The leatherback sea turtle can weigh over 2,000 pounds (900 kg)!

Turtle Shells

Turtles are the only reptiles with shells. Shells come in many shapes and colors.

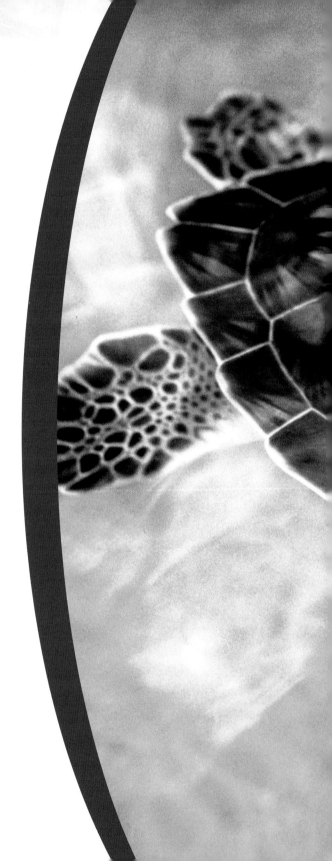

A turtle's shell is like a **shield**. It **protects** the turtle from **predators**.

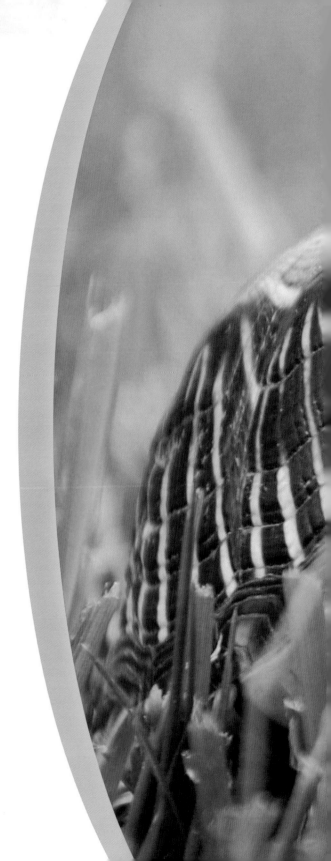

Baby Turtles

Both sea and land turtles lay their eggs on land. A female digs a nest with her back feet.

19

The female covers her
eggs with dirt and leaves.
Baby turtles are on their
own after they hatch.

More Facts

- It is believed that turtles have been around for millions of years. That makes them one of the oldest living animals on Earth.

- For most turtles, the temperature of the nest will decide whether turtles are girls or boys. Warmer temperatures make girls, while cooler temperatures make boys.

- Land turtles are very slow. They can only walk about 0.5 mph (0.8 km/h). But the leatherback sea turtle can swim 22 mph (35 km/h). That is pretty fast!

Glossary

cold-blooded – reptiles and fishes whose blood temperature changes with the outside temperature.

freshwater – water that does not have salt in it like oceans do.

habitat – a place where a living thing is naturally found.

hatch – to be born from an egg.

predator – an animal that lives by eating other animals.

protect – keep safe from harm.

scales – flat plates that form the outer covering of reptiles.

shield – an object that keeps one safe from harm.

swamp – wet land that is filled with trees and/or other plants.

Index

babies 20

eggs 18, 20

habitat 6, 8

nest 18

predator 16

reptile 4, 14

sea turtle 8, 18

shell 14, 16

size 10, 12

abdokids.com

Use this code to log on to abdokids.com and access crafts, games, videos and more!

Abdo Kids Code:

RTK0625